SELECTED PIANO WORKS

OF

HELEN C. CRANE

BOOK THREE

Bernard R. Crane

Editor

ISBN 978-1-7358882-9-3
BISAC: MUS037090
LOC Classification: M6 – 175.5

Helen C. Crane in her mid 20's (c. 1890)
enhanced photograph of Helen C. Crane as pictured in the publication
"The Music Monitor" July. 1919 – Vol. VIII, No. 10

SELECTED PIANO WORKS OF

HELEN C. CRANE

TABLE OF CONTENTS

BOOK THREE

Two Intermezzi

No. 1

Helen C. Crane
Op. 38 , no. 1

**Allegro non troppo
ma appassionato**

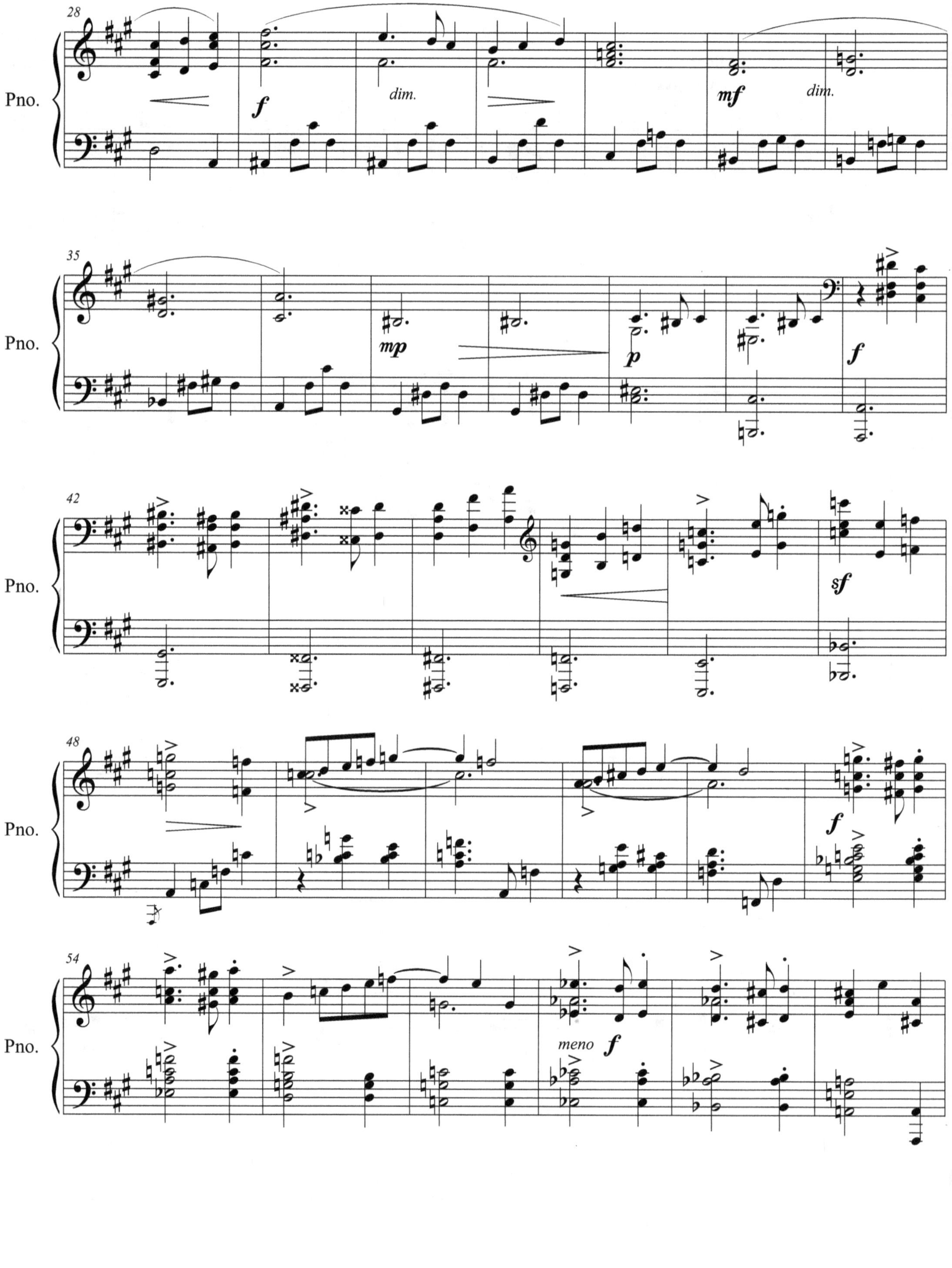
28
Pno.
dim.
dim.
35
Pno.
42
Pno.
48
Pno.
54
Pno.
meno

Helen C. Crane

Two Intermezzi

Op. 38, no. 1

94
Pno.
cresc.
f
mp
mf
mp
100
Pno.
mf
105
Pno.
mf
p
111
Pno.
p
cresc.
116
Pno.
mp
mf

Helen C. Crane

Two Intermezzi

Op. 38, no. 1

149
rit.
a tempo
Pno.
dim.
154
cresc.
159
rit.
Allegro moderato
166
173
rinf.

Helen C. Crane

Two Intermezzi

Op. 38, no. 1

213
Pno.
meno
f
219
dim.
mf
226
232
sf
mf
dim.
poco rit.
239
mp
dim.
p
pp
poco tranquillo

Helen C. Crane   Two Intermezzi   Op. 38, no. 1

Four Character Pieces

No. 1

Wanderlust

Helen C. Crane

Op.6, no.1

Piano

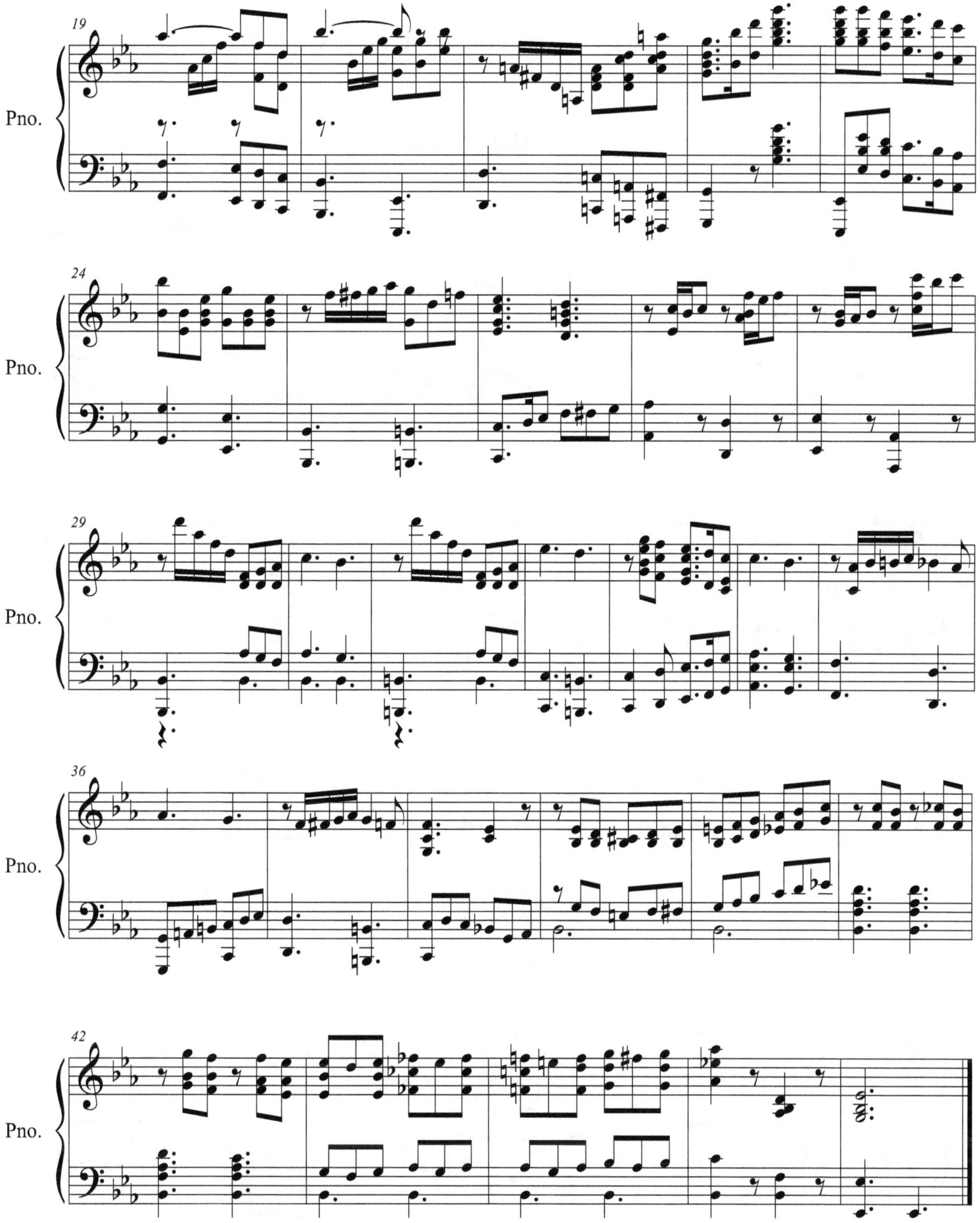
19
Pno.
24
Pno.
29
Pno.
36
Pno.
42
Pno.

Four Character Pieces

No. 2

Waldestille

Helen C. Crane
Op.6, no.2

34
Pno.
cresc.
f
41
Pno.
mf
cresc.
ff
allargando
49
a tempo
rit.
a tempo
Pno.
dim.
57
Pno.
mf
65
Pno.
dim.
pp

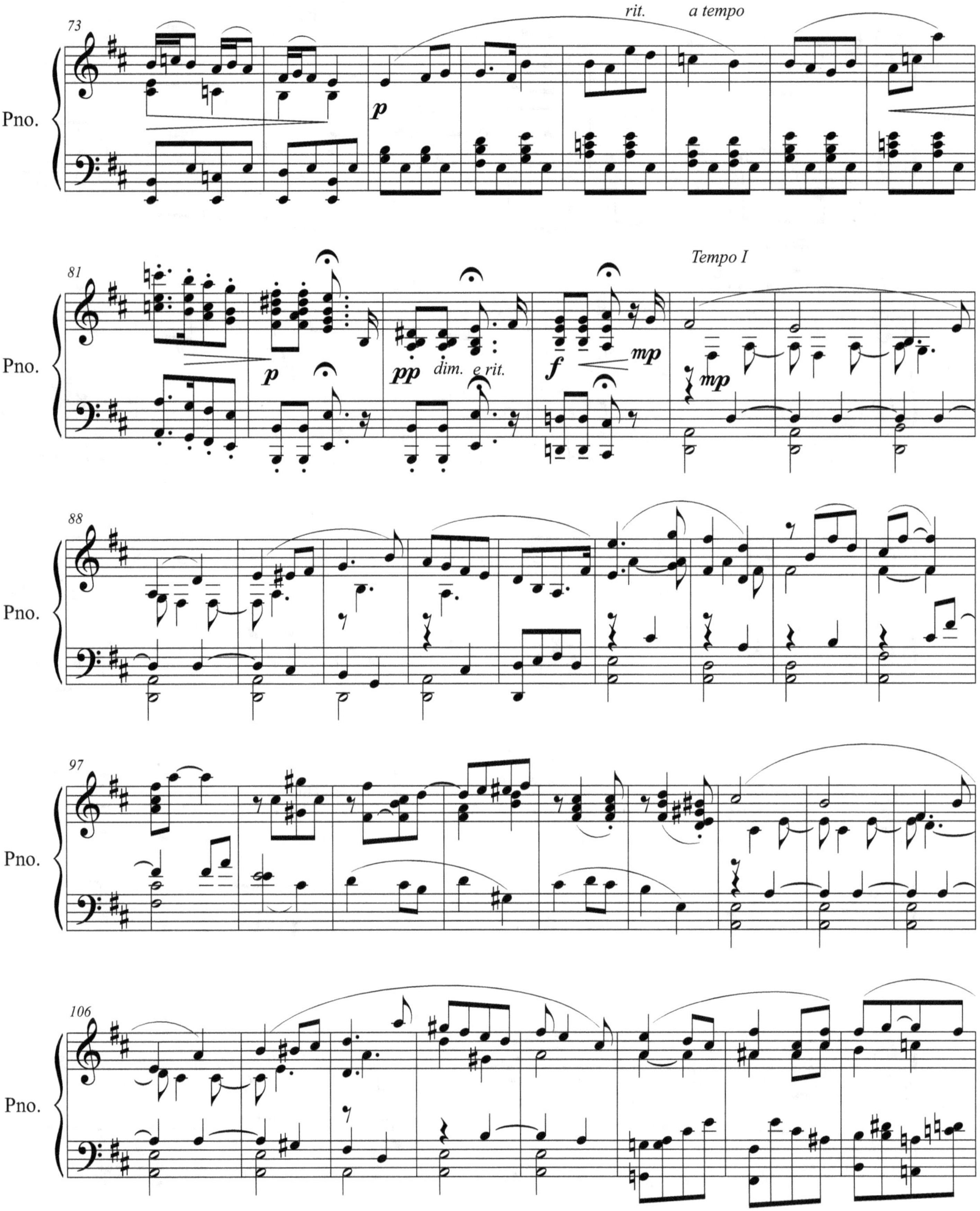
73
rit.
a tempo
Pno.
p
81
Tempo I
p
pp
dim. e rit.
f
mp
mp
88
97
106

H.C. Crane

Waldstille

Op. 6, no.2

Four Character Pieces

No. 3

Über Alle Berge

Helen C. Crane
Op.6, no.3

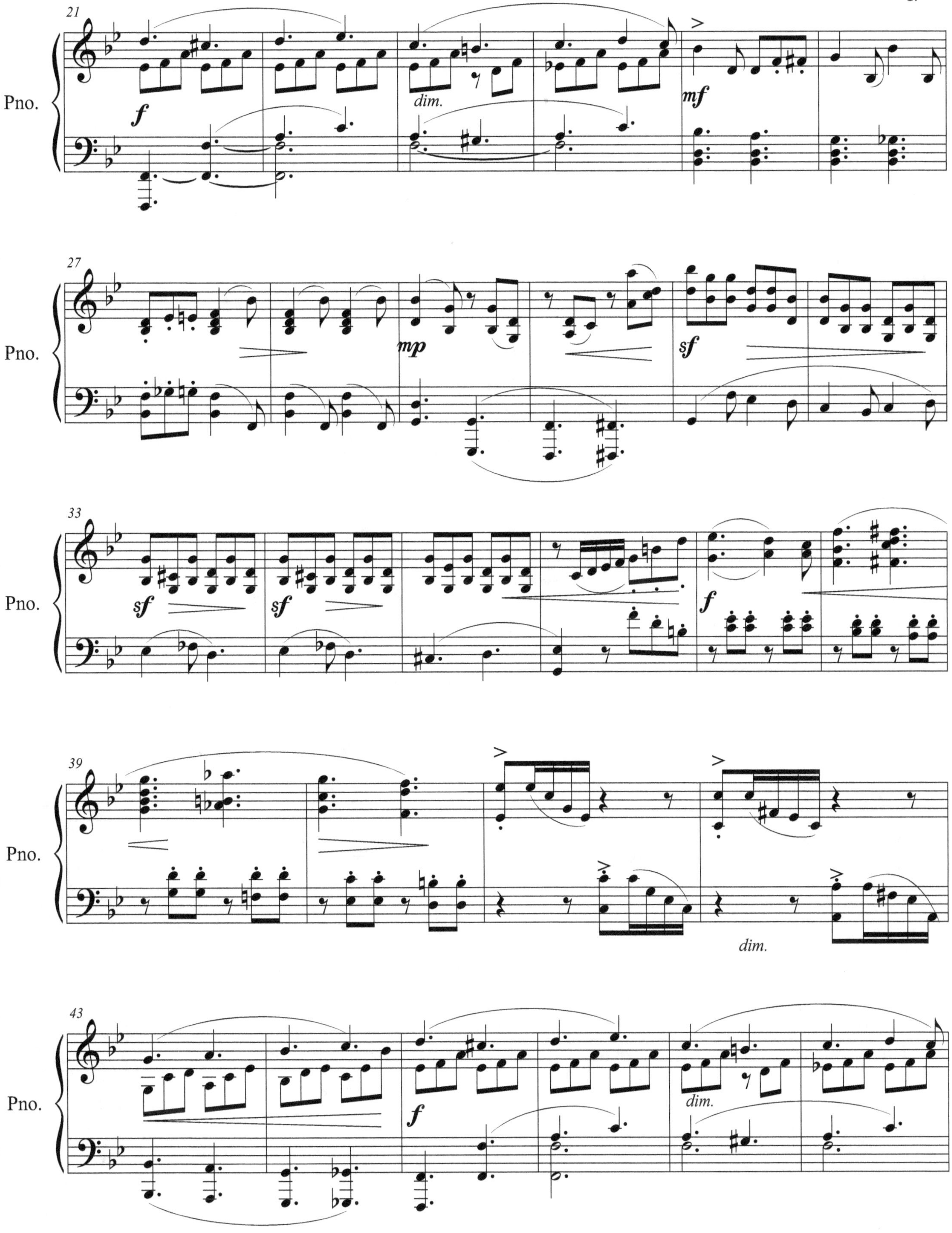
21
Pno.
f
dim.
mf
27
Pno.
mp
sf
33
Pno.
sf
sf
f
39
Pno.
dim.
43
Pno.
f
dim.

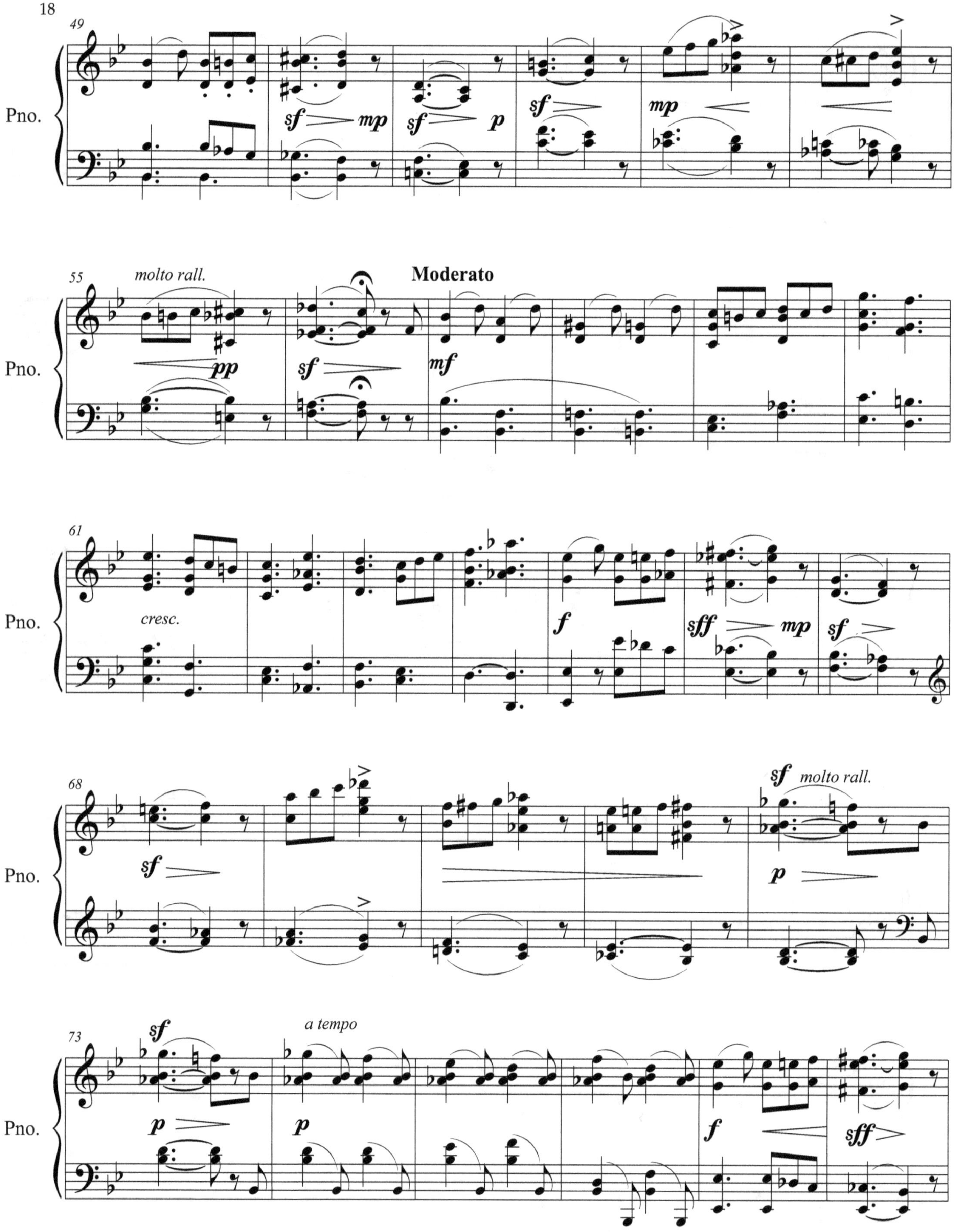
Pno.
molto rall.
Moderato
cresc.
molto rall.
a tempo

Helen C. Crane

Uber Alle Berge

Pno.
dim.
Pno.
Pno.
cresc.
poco rit.
Pno.
a tempo
dolce tranquillo
Pno.

Helen C. Crane

Uber Alle Berge

Four Character Pieces

No. 4

Herzenrast

Helen C. Crane

Op.6, no.4

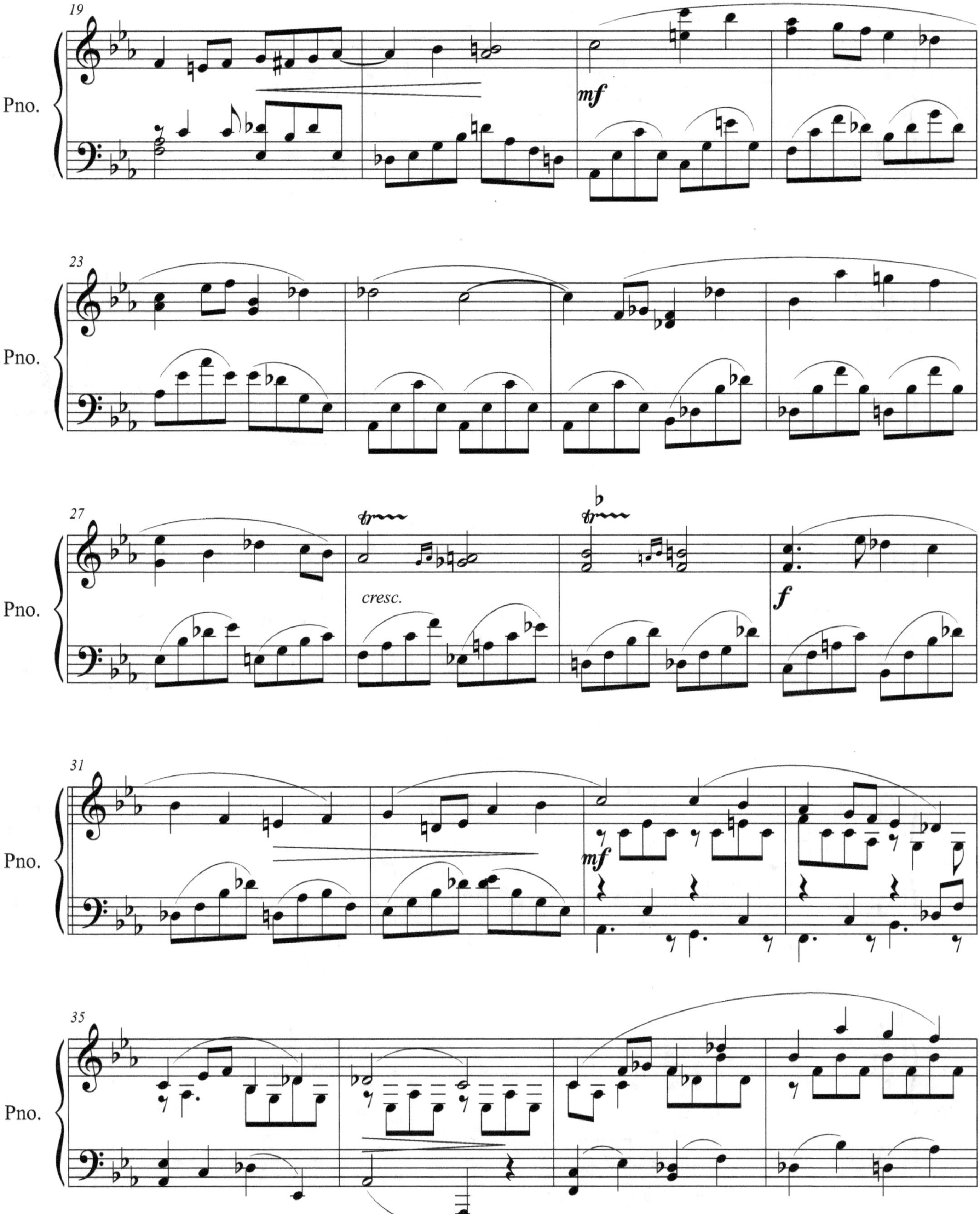

19
Pno.
mf
23
Pno.
27
Pno.
cresc.
f
31
Pno.
mf
35
Pno.

39
Pno.
cresc.
44
Pno.
f
ff
49
Pno.
pp
54
Pno.
pp
mp
60
Pno.
poco cresc.
dim.
rall.

Helen C. Crane

Herzenrast

Op. 6, no.4

Allegro leggierissimo

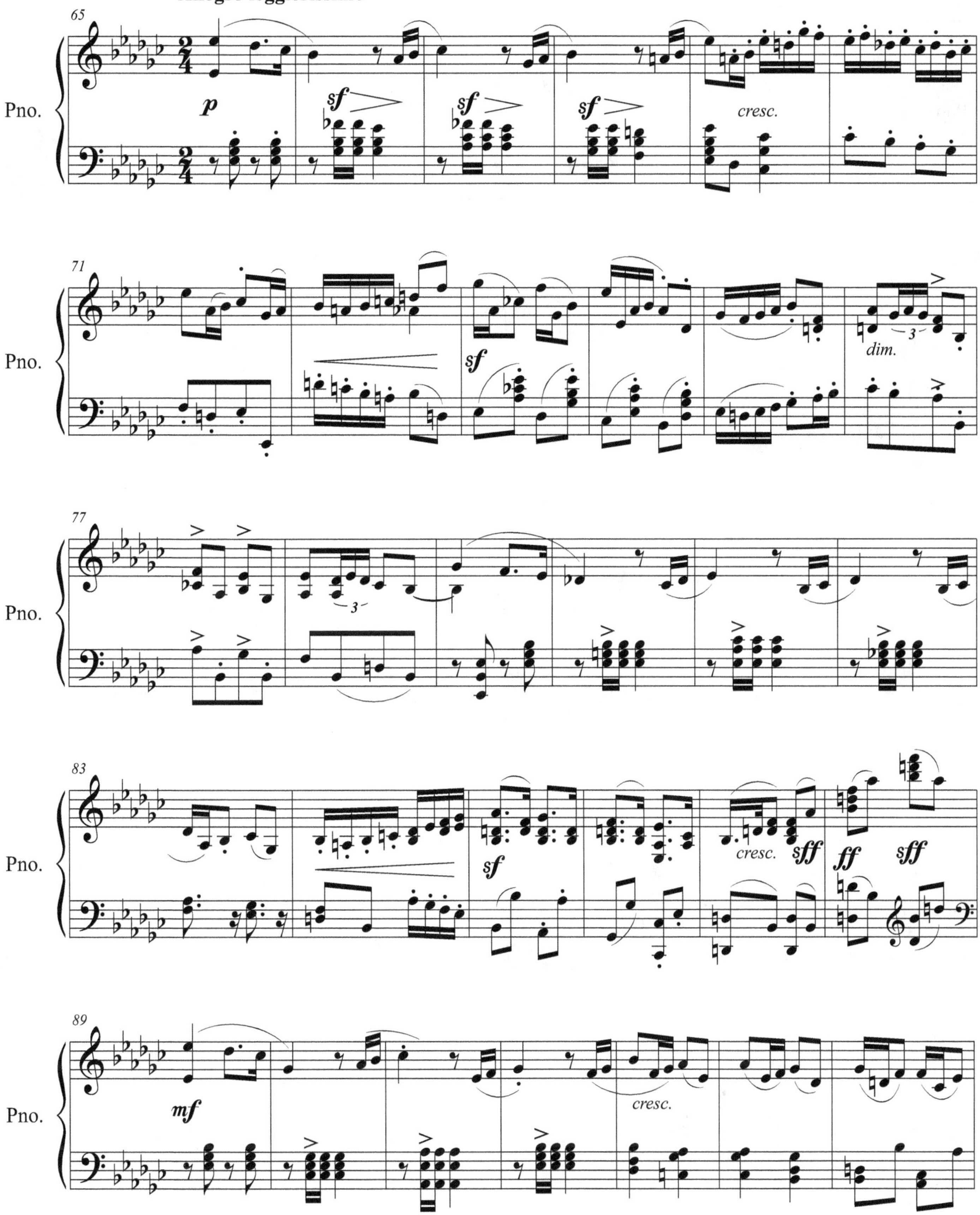

96
Pno.
f
p
102
Pno.
cresc.
108
Pno.
dim.
3
114
Pno.
p
riten. molto
Tempo I
120
Pno.
p
poco cresc.

125
Pno.
dim.
dolce
p
130
Pno.
cresc.
mf
f
134
Pno.
cresc.
sff
139
Pno.
p
rit.
143
Pno.
pp
pp

Scènes Champêtres

No. 1

Helen C. Crane

Op. 31, no.1

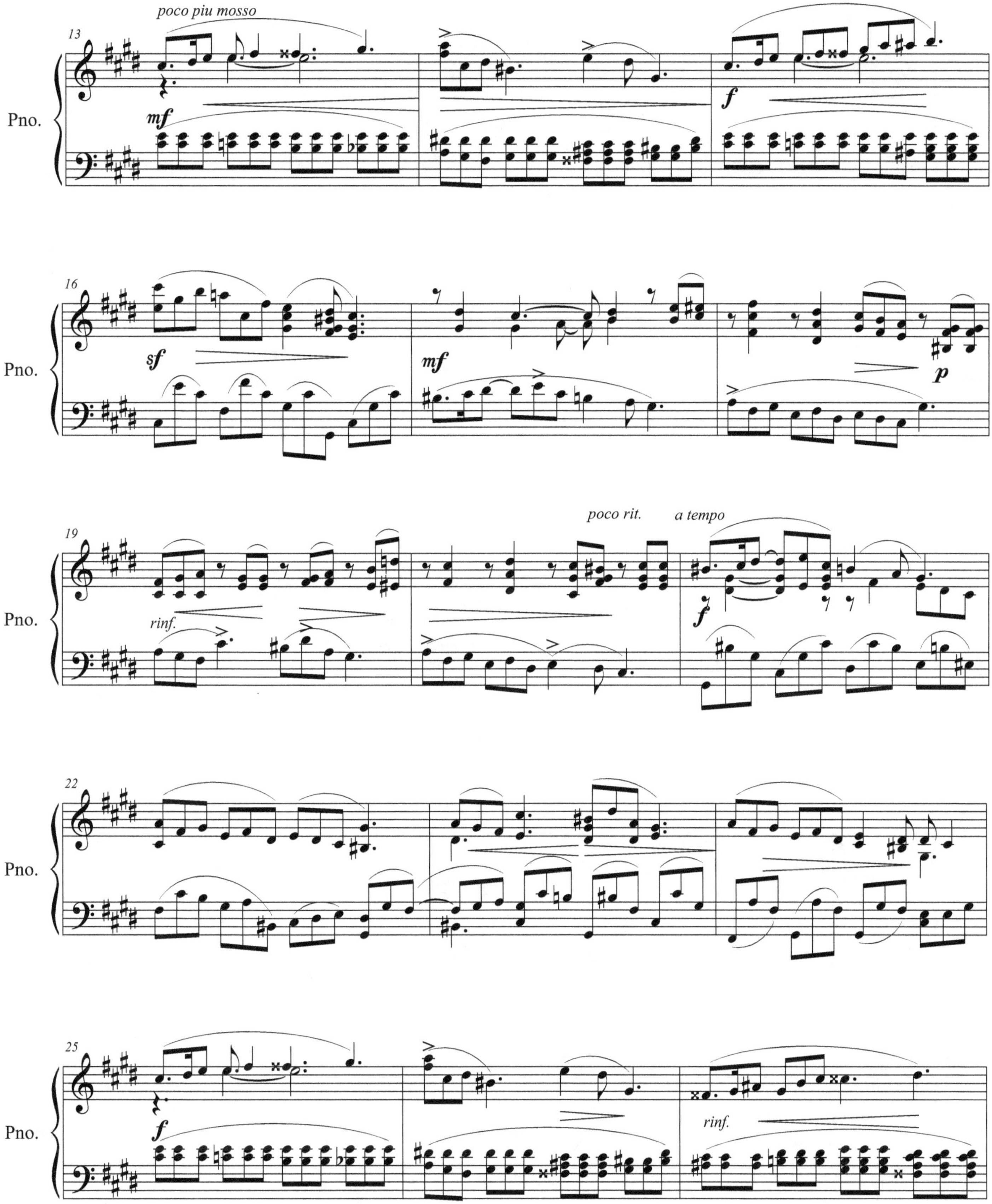
poco piu mosso
Pno.
mf
f
sf
p
rinf.
poco rit.
a tempo

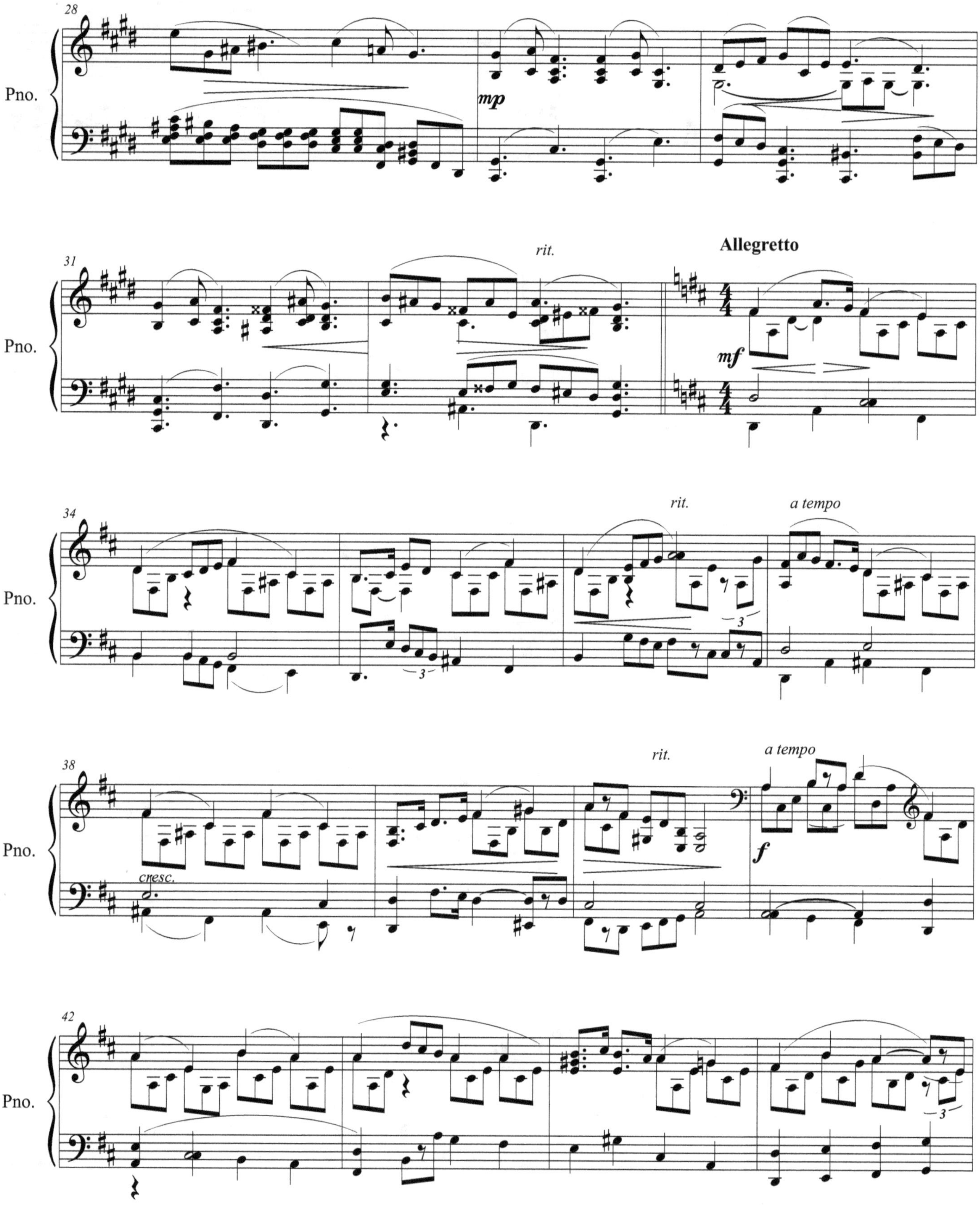
Pno.
mp
rit.
Allegretto
mf
rit.
a tempo
cresc.
rit.
a tempo
f

46
poco largo
a tempo
Pno.
3
50
rit.
a tempo
Pno.
3
3
54
rit.
a tempo
Pno.
3
3
cresc.
58
Pno.
3
f
poco string.
62
poco rit.
a tempo
Pno.
p
poco largo
3
3

66
rit.
a tempo
Pno.
3
70
cresc.
rit.
sf
74
ff
sf
79
rit.
f
Tempo I
mp
82
poco piu mosso

Helen C. Crane

Scènes Champêtres

No. 2

Helen C. Crane

Op. 31, no. 2

28
Pno.
35
rit.
a tempo
Pno.
43
rit.
a tempo
Pno.
meno f
50
Pno.
dim.
57
Pno.
cresc.

63
rit.
Pno.
f
dim.
70
a tempo
Pno.
pp
76
Pno.
cresc.
f
82
Pno.
89
rit.
Pno.
p

a tempo
rit.
a tempo
Pno.
rit.
a tempo
p
rit.
a tempo
cresc.
f
rit.
tranquillo
e ben legato
cresc.
mf
rit.
a tempo
cresc.
sf
f

133
Pno.
141
Pno.
p
149
Pno.
piu f
157
Pno.
cresc.
f
marc.
165
Pno.
rit.
a tempo
f

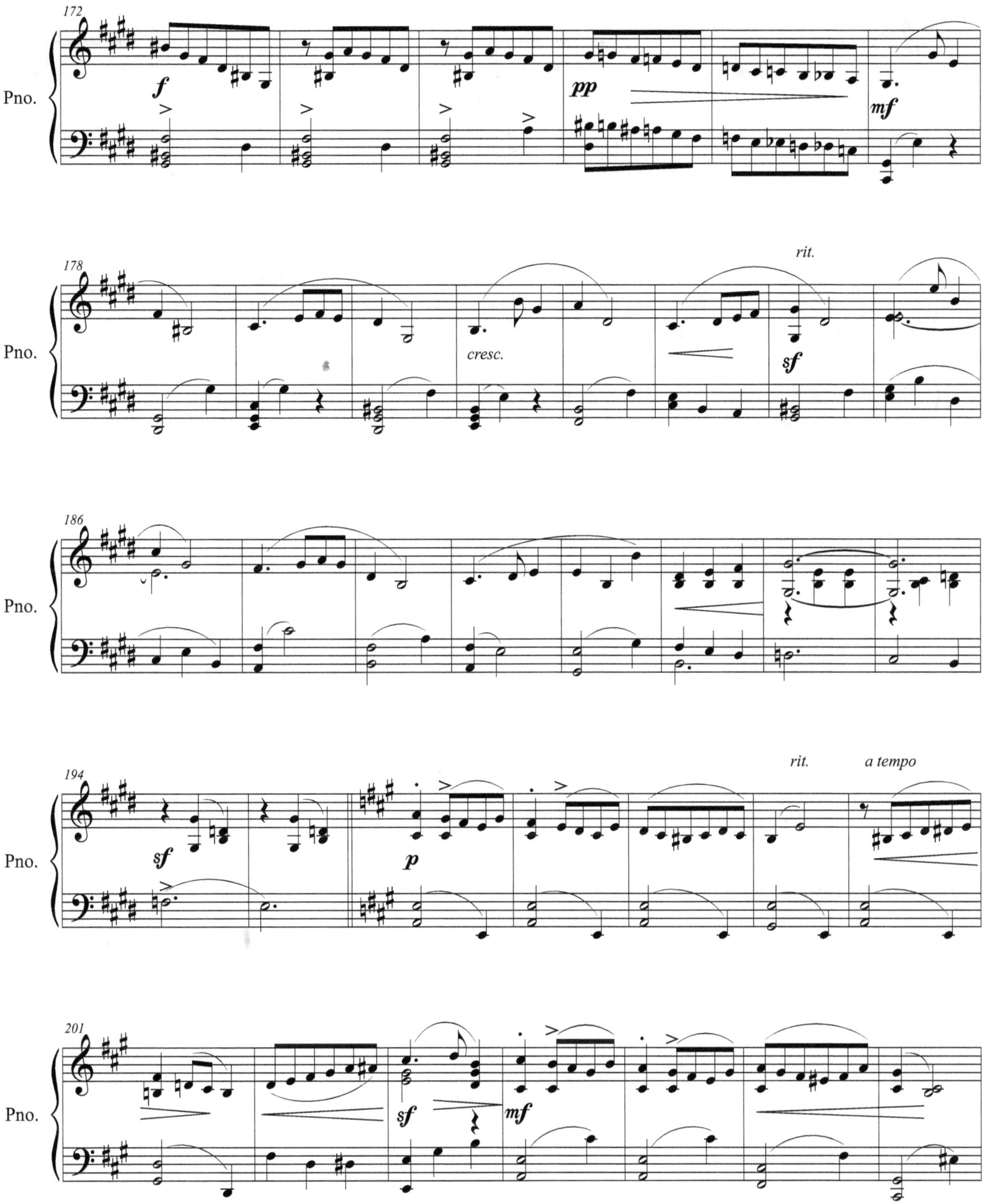
172
Pno.
f
pp
mf
178
rit.
cresc.
sf
186
194
rit.
a tempo
sf
p
201
sf
mf

208
rit.
a tempo
Pno.
pp
215
rit.
a tempo
poco stringendo
8va
Pno.
223
Pno.

Scènes Champêtres

No. 3

Helen C. Crane

Op. 31, no.3

Lento con molto sentimento

33
Pno.
sff
mp
marc.
p
p
41
Pno.
rit.
rallentando
p
p
pp
sf
51
Pno.
pp
mp
58
Pno.
poco cresc.
mf
64
Pno.
rit.
a tempo
mp

Helen C. Crane

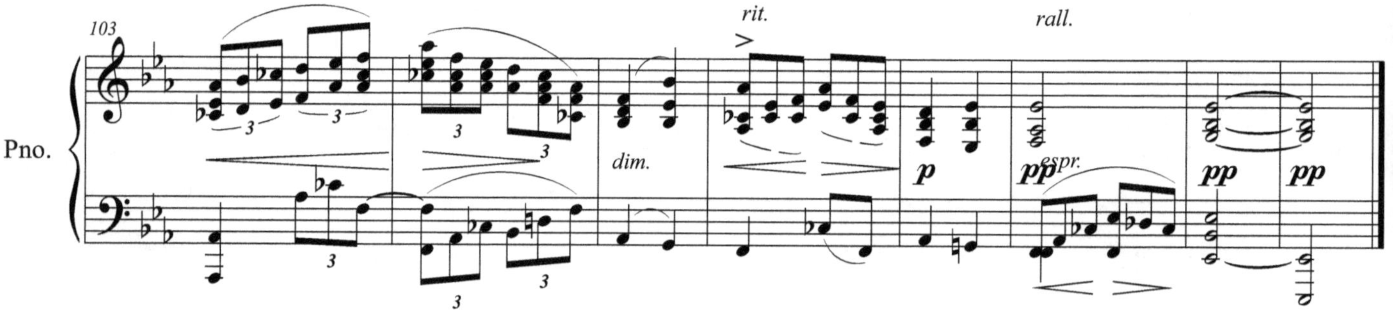
103
Pno.
rit.
rall.
dim.
p
pp
espr.
pp
pp

Scènes Champêtres

No. 4

Helen C. Crane

Op. 31, no.4

19
rit.
a tempo
Pno.
mp
mf
24
Pno.
sf
29
Pno.
cresc.
sf
f
34
rit.
a tempo
Pno.
f
dim.
p
f
39
rit.
a tempo
Pno.
p
f

Helen C. Crane

**Lo stesso tempo
ma un poco tranquillo**

95
rit.
a tempo
rit.
mp
Pno.
101
a tempo
rinf.
ff
106
rit.
a tempo
dim.
piu f
111
dim.
p
dim.
116
pp
f

121
Pno.
rit.
a tempo
dim.
piu f
126
Pno.
dim.
p
dim.
131
Pno.
pp
136
molto rit.
a tempo
rit.
a tempo
Pno.
mp
f
142
Pno.
mf

Helen C. Crane

173
Pno.
cresc.
sf
f
178
Pno.
f
rit.
dim.
a tempo
p
f
184
Pno.
rit.
a tempo
f
189
Pno.
rit.
a tempo
p
195
Pno.
p
p
mf

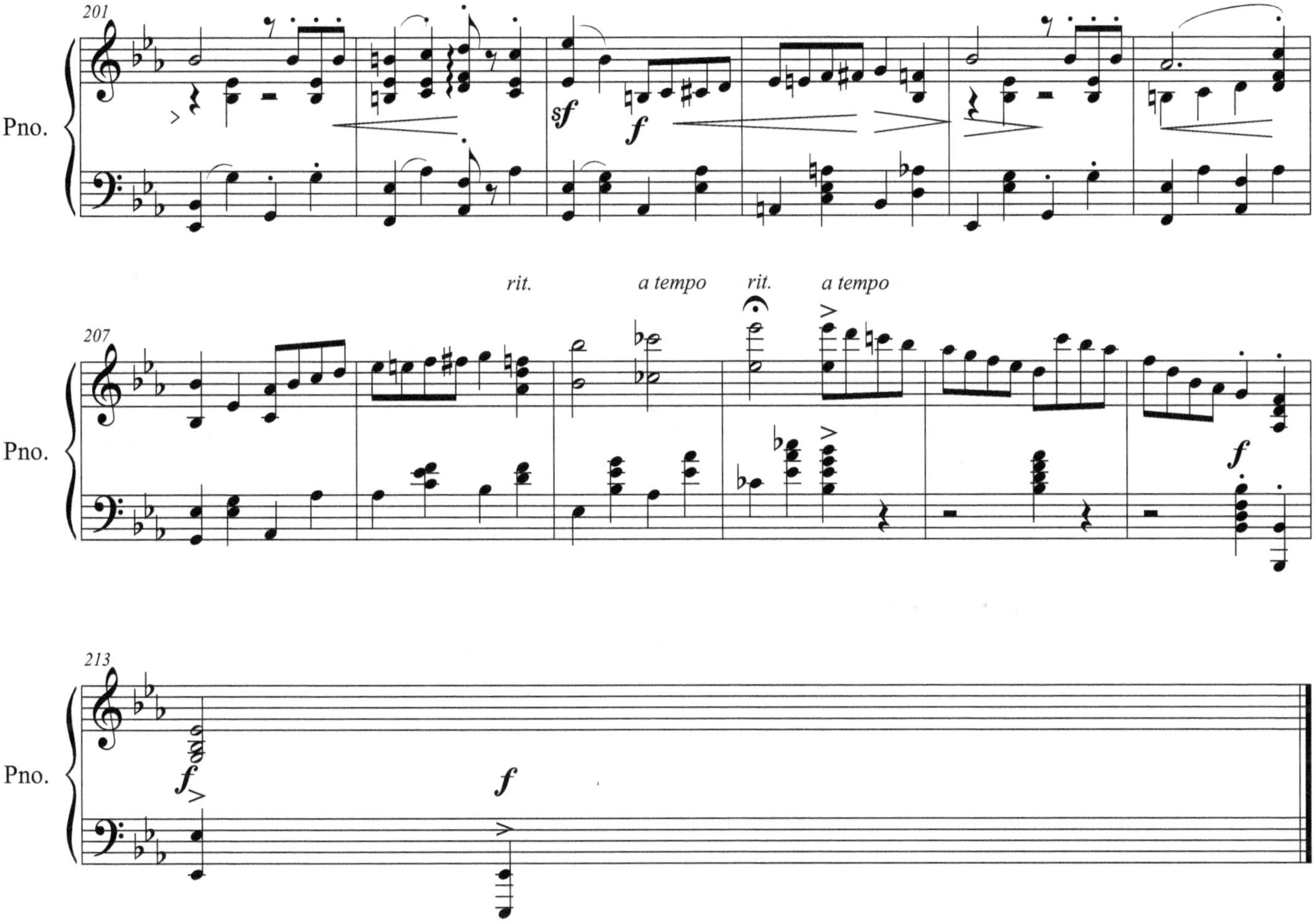
201
Pno.
sf
f
207
rit.
a tempo
rit.
a tempo
f
213
f
f

Scènes Champêtres

No. 5

Helen C. Crane

Op. 31, no.5

Non troppo lento con gran espressione

26
Pno.
32
poco rit.
a tempo
39
poco largo
rall.
poco moderato
dolce
45
marc.
51
rinf.

56
Pno.
molto espressivo
meno
60
rit.
a tempo
molto dim.
66
rit.
dim.
molto cresc.
72
Tempo I
78
poco largo
a tempo
cresc.

85
rallentando
a tempo
Pno.
molto dim.
p
92
poco stringendo
a tempo
ritenuto
rinf.
99
poco stringendo
mf
cresc.
f
105
poco rit.
a tempo
f
111
poco largo
mf

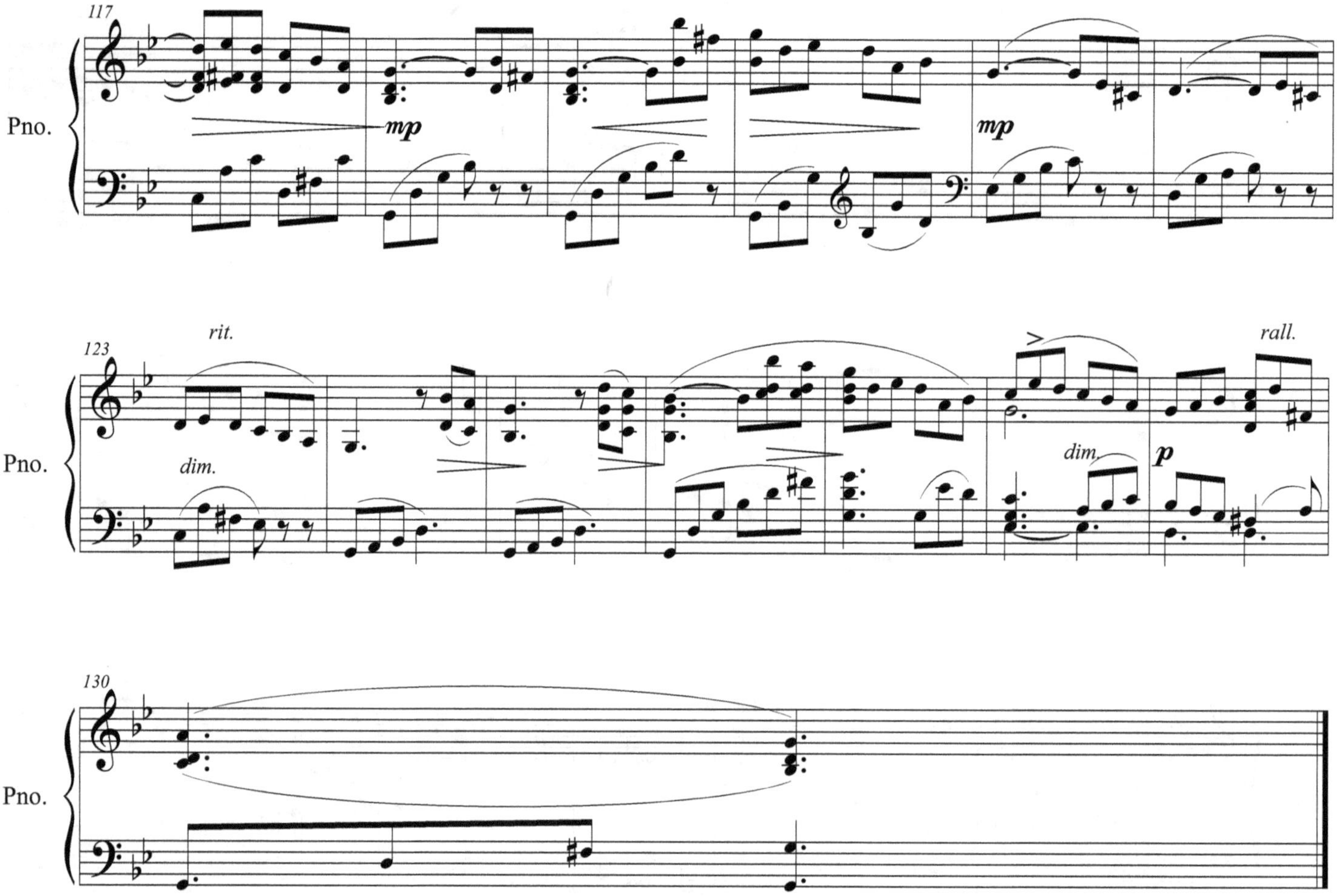
117
Pno.
mp
mp
123
rit.
dim.
Pno.
dim.
p
rall.
130
Pno.

Scènes Champêtres

No. 6

Helen C. Crane

Op. 31, no.6

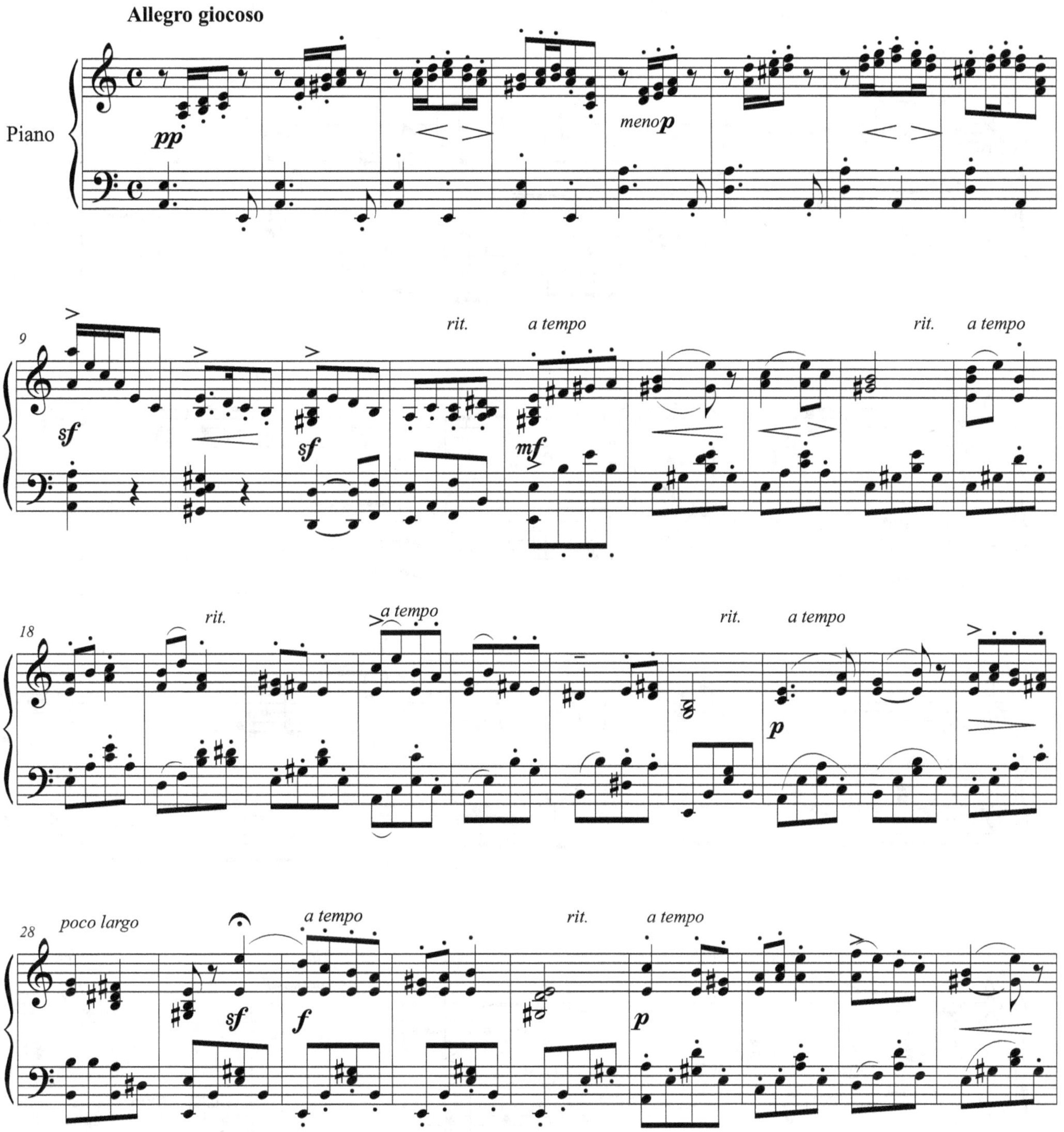

60

Helen C. Crane

62

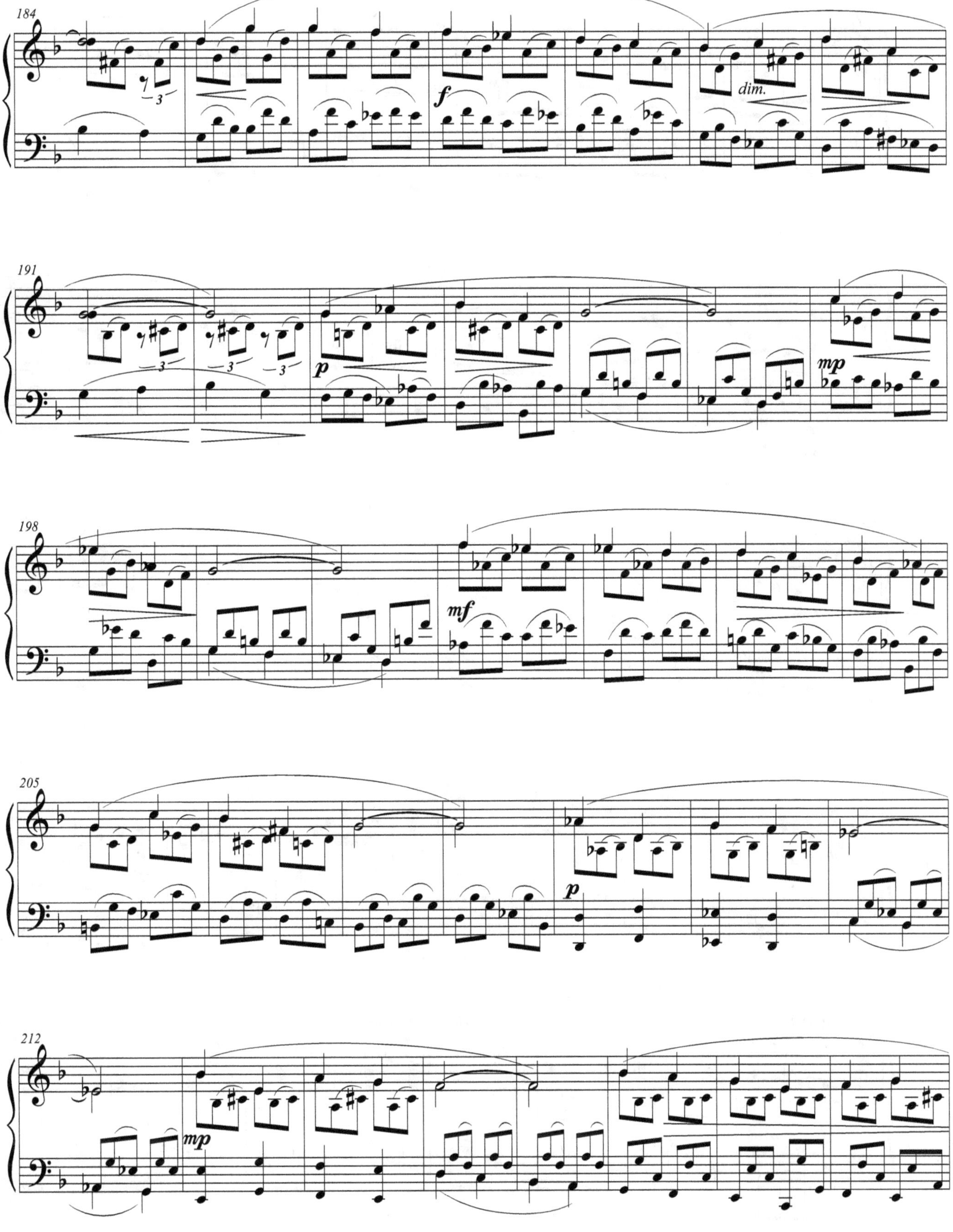
184
Pno.
f
dim.
191
Pno.
p
mp
198
Pno.
mf
205
Pno.
p
212
Pno.
mp

220
Pno.
p
mf
227
Pno.
3
cresc.
234
Allegro giocoso
Pno.
f
pp
241
rit.
Pno.
meno p
sf
sf
249
a tempo
rit.
a tempo
rit.
a tempo
Pno.
mf

258
rit.
a tempo
poco largo
a tempo
Pno.
p
sf
f
267
rit.
a tempo
Pno.
p
f
sf
276
rit.
a tempo
Pno.
mf
sf
285
Pno.
f
sf
sf
295
rit.
rit.
Pno.
mf

304
a tempo
Pno.
cresc.
dim.
cresc.
314
rit.
Tempo I
8va
sf
mf
piu f
323
(8va)
sf
f
ff
ff

September Days

No. 1

Helen C. Crane

Op. 62, no.1

68

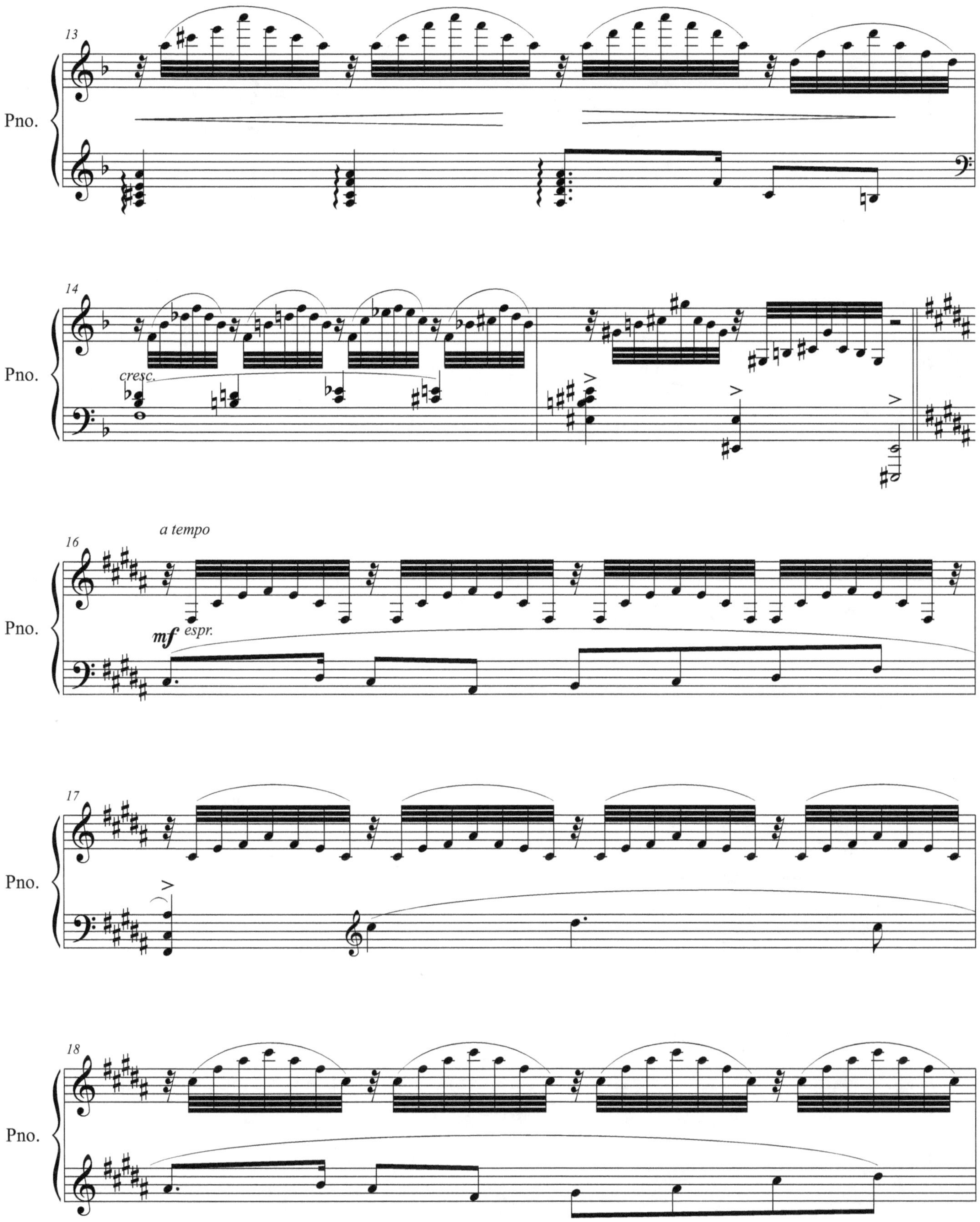
13
Pno.
14
Pno.
cresc.
16
a tempo
Pno.
mf espr.
17
Pno.
18
Pno.

Pno.
un poco affrettandosi
rit.
a tempo
perpendosi
dim.
dolce espr.
e ben legato
rit.
a tempo
poco cresc.

Helen C. Crane

53
Pno.
p
cresc.
57
rit.
a tempo
rit.
a tempo
Pno.
dim.
p
piu p
61
rit.
a tempo
Pno.
dim.
mf
63
Pno.
64
Pno.

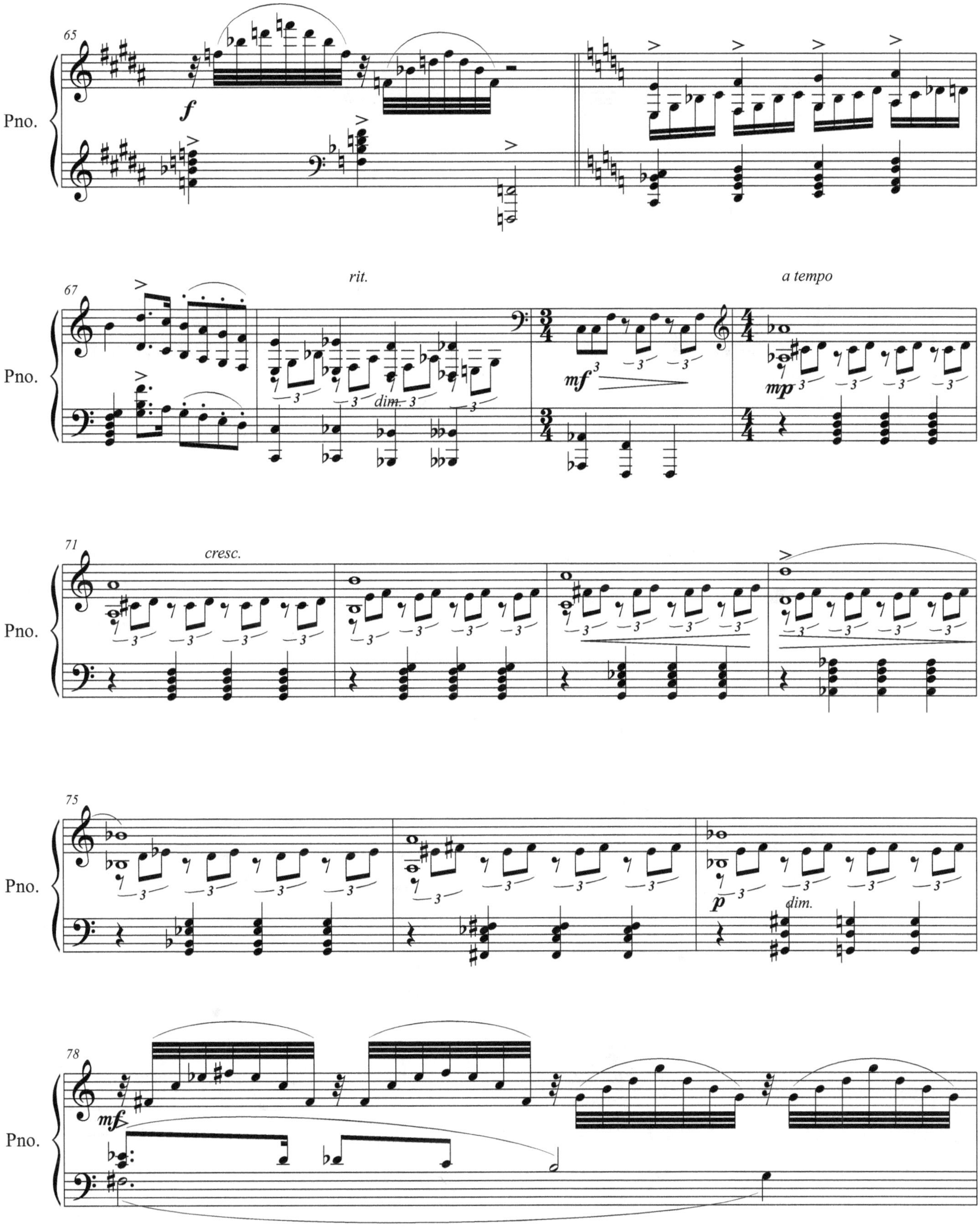
65
Pno.
f
67
rit.
a tempo
mf
dim.
mp
71
cresc.
75
p
dim.
78
mf

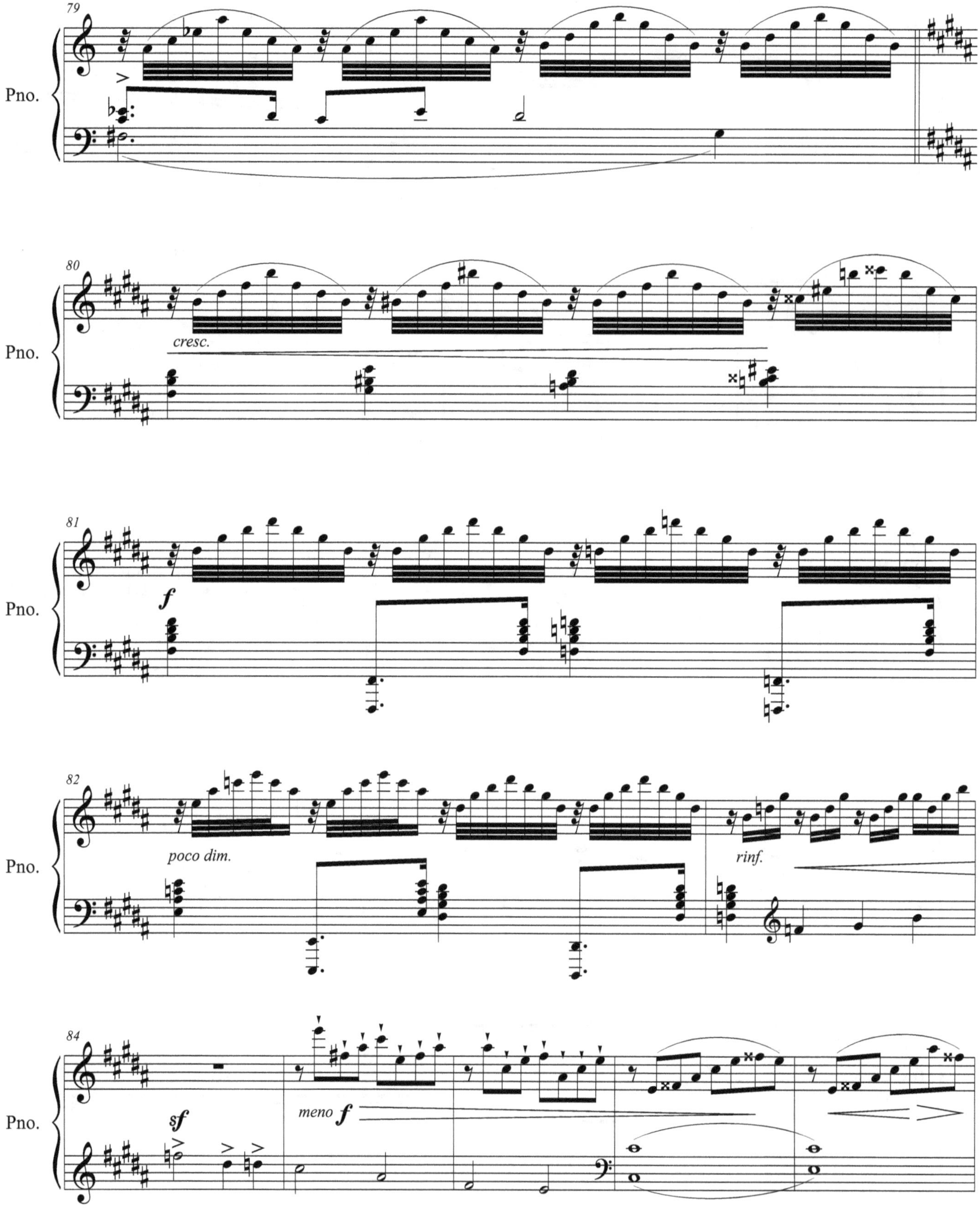
79
Pno.
80
Pno.
cresc.
81
Pno.
f
82
Pno.
poco dim.
rinf.
84
Pno.
sf
meno f

Charlottenburg
23 January 1920

September Days

No. 2

Helen C. Crane
Op. 62, no.2

24
Pno.
p
cresc.
32
Pno.
rit.
a tempo
mf
cresc.
f
p
39
rit.
a tempo
Pno.
pp
p
mf
46
Pno.
poco allargando
51
Pno.
a tempo
dim.

56
Pno.
rinf.
R.H.
61
a tempo
p
cresc.
69
animandosi
f
77
84
Andante
p
pp
dolce espr.

92
Pno.
p
100
Pno.
pp
107
Pno.
115
Pno.
mp
122
poco piu animato
Pno.
mf
cresc.

Charlottenburg, Germany
29 January 1920

September Days

No. 3

Helen C. Crane

Op. 62, no.3

26
rit.
Pno.
rinf.
espr.
dim.
33
a tempo
39
rit.
con tenderezza
a tempo
con fuoco
f
sf
45
dim.
52
mf

Helen C. Crane

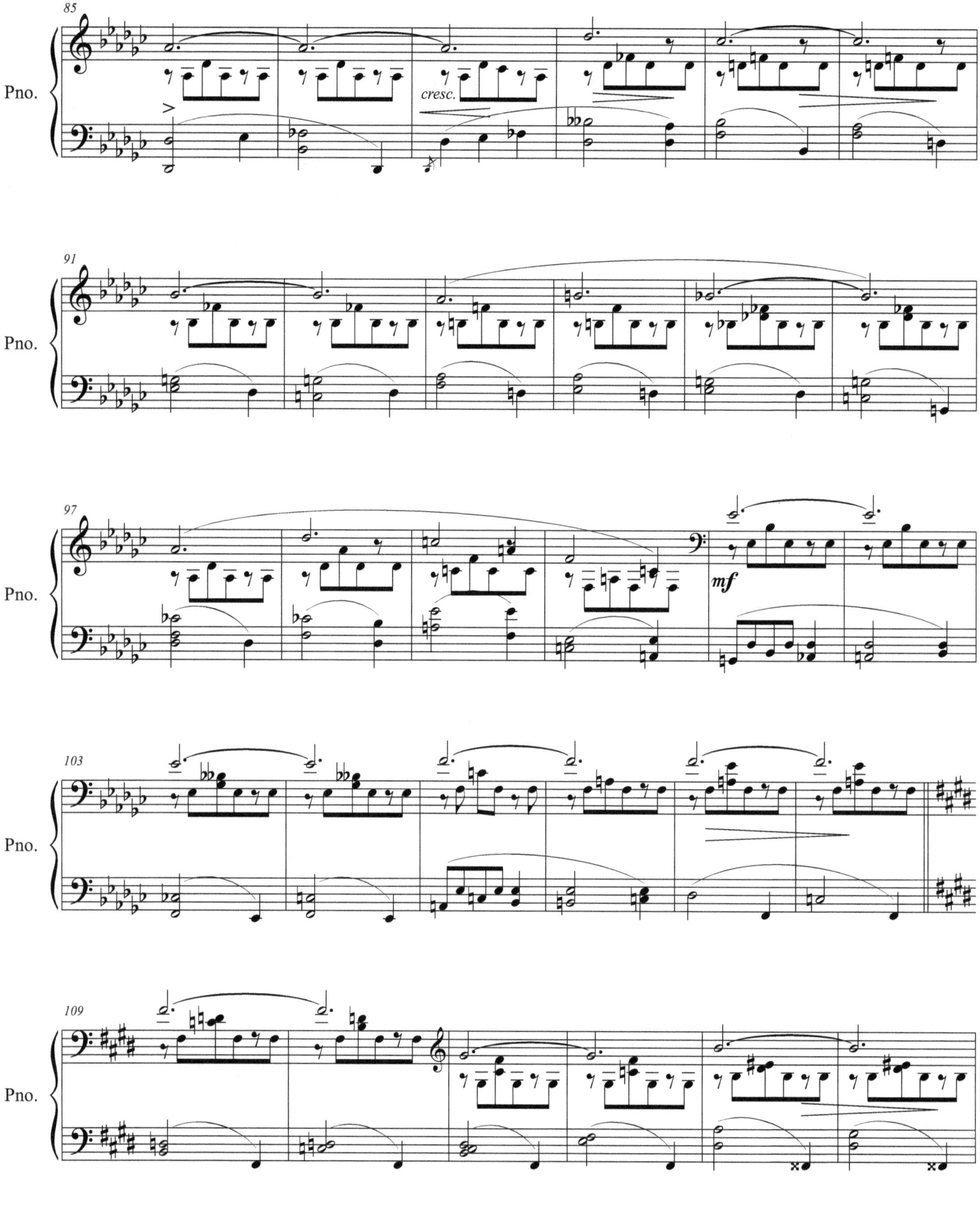
85
Pno.
cresc.
91
Pno.
97
Pno.
mf
103
Pno.
109
Pno.

Helen C. Crane

September Days - No. 3   Op.62, no.3

Charlottenburg, Germany
2 February 1920

www.ingramcontent.com/pod-product-compliance
Lightning Source LLC
Chambersburg PA
CBHW062032090426
42733CB00034B/2594